Through the Storms

Charleston, SC
www.PalmettoPublishing.com

Through the Storms
Copyright © 2022 by Senedtra Cowan

Hardcover ISBN: 979-8-8229-0813-0
Paperback ISBN: 979-8-8229-0814-7
eBook ISBN: 979-8-8229-0815-4

Through the Storms

Hurricane Irma and Hurricane Maria

Senedtra Cowan

Preface

In 2017, I was living and working in the US Virgin Islands until we were hit by two powerful hurricanes. After I returned home to Alabama, some people seemed to have various opinions about my experience. Some church members saw it as a great opportunity for a testimony. Some were inspired by my courage. Some were more intrigued by the details of my journey and wanted to know more. I encouraged other people who had decided to remain in the US Virgin Islands to write about their experiences. Some people stateside asked why I didn't do the same. I responded that I thought natives or current residents should be the ones to write about their experiences. I decided to go ahead and start writing about my experience in Saint Thomas, but I went through a period of procrastination until one day the Holy Spirit spoke to me and told me to finish and publish this book. Now is the time, so here it goes…

Table of Contents

Figure 1 : Senedtra and Lexi

Chapter One

Going to the VI

Although I had earned a master's degree, in 2014, I accepted an entry-level position as a mail clerk as a way to get my foot in the door. My supervisors understood and were realistic; they encouraged my coworkers and me to apply for other jobs as they were advertised. During 2016, I became very persistent and aggressive in my search, but all I achieved was a lateral move. I really was not getting anywhere in advancing my career.

I experienced a lot of financial hardship. I was earning enough to stay off welfare but not enough to cover expenses such as a car repair or an unexpectedly high electric bill. It turned into a game of borrowing from one merchant to pay the other. I began to pray. I asked God to please help me provide for my two-year-old daughter, so I did not have to struggle from one paycheck to the next.

One day I was chatting with an ex from my undergraduate years of college. He observed how hard I had worked for my bachelor's degree and how I had gone on to earn a master's degree, and he threw in my face how he had opted out of college and was earning more money than me.

Instead of snapping, which I was tempted to do, I bit my tongue and said to myself, "No, I'm not going to hate on him. I'm going to take this and somehow learn from it."

So I said to him, "Yeah, I remember. Would you mind sharing your keys to success?"

He said one thing that made a light bulb go on in my head. He calmly said, "Senedtra, you have to learn to be flexible."

Something told me that I needed to consider his advice, hold on tight to it, and try it. I continued job hunting and became even more aggressive. Every day during my fifteen-minute breaks, I was clicking buttons on the computer to apply for jobs like there was no tomorrow.

One day I saw a position I was very interested in. It offered good promotional opportunities in a relatively short period of time. However, it stated the position was in Saint Thomas and Saint Croix, VI. I grew excited. I had visited Washington DC, several times, and I envisioned walking down the street in a suit, carrying a briefcase, going to change the world for the better. Later that day, it occurred to me that something was off about the location "VI," but I brushed it off, thinking it was probably a typo.

A few weeks later, I received a call. The caller introduced himself and said, "You applied for the position in Saint Croix and Saint Thomas, US Virgin Islands."

I thought to myself, "I did?!"

He continued, "We reviewed many applications and were very impressed with your résumé. We would like to interview you. Are you still interested?"

I paused and thought, "That is so far away, and I don't know where it is on the map!" Then I heard my ex's voice say, "Senedtra, you have to learn to be flexible."

So I enthusiastically responded, "Yes!"

I wondered if this opportunity would be my breakthrough. The caller told me the time and date for the phone interview and ended the call. I felt excited and so ignorant at the same time because I had mixed up VI—the abbreviation for the US Virgin Islands—with VA, the abbreviation for the state of Virginia. It was not my fault; US territories were never discussed in my social studies classes.

About a month after the interview, I was offered the position on Saint Thomas. I was excited and felt like I'd hit the jackpot. I thought it would be a great opportunity to advance in my career in a relatively short period of time and, of course, provide a higher quality of life for my child. Her well-being was what drove me to move forward when I didn't even want to do things for myself. I took a few weeks to prepare for departure. I closed accounts and informed merchants, as well as family and friends, of my relocation. My supervisor and manager expressed how proud they were that one of their employees was selected for a great opportunity.

As I was looking out of the window while the airplane was landing, the scene before me was beyond beautiful. I was so in awe of God's creation that it took my breath away. I turned to the passenger next to me and said, "Blue has been my favorite color for twenty years, but I think I have a new favorite color now."

The passenger asked, "What color did it change to?"

I looked out the window and pointed at the water. "Turquoise. Wow! I mean, this place looks just like the postcards."

The passenger who I was talking to leaned over toward me and said a few times, "Breathe."

When we landed and I walked into the airport, there was a big horizontal banner that stated, "Welcome to America's Paradise!" I was not a drinker (and still am not), but all the tourists were offered a complimentary shot of rum. I'd never tried rum before. I was curious and asked how it tasted. They told me to pick a flavor. I looked at the options, and there were about ten fruity flavors. I thought if I was going to brag about trying rum one day, I should get the real deal—from the island—so I tried one and handled it well. I didn't choke and embarrass myself in front of the server. It had a nice flavor. Then I looked for a cab with baggage service and headed for the hotel.

During the first few months, there was a lot to learn in addition to job training. Outside of work, I had to learn how to drive on the left side of the road. I had to get familiar with different dialects, customs, and the proper etiquette within the new culture. I already knew how to float, but I thought it would be helpful to know how to swim. As I was getting acquainted with people on the island, I met a very confident former FBI agent who assured me that he could teach me how to swim very quickly.

Figure 2: My Studio Apartment before Hurricane Irma

We decided on a time to meet at the beach. He was right. I learned how to swim during the first session!

It took a while to get acclimated to the island, but eventually I found a place that I was happy with and that was suitable for my daughter. We had a community pool that had a view that overlooked the Atlantic Ocean, and I thought it was pretty cool to be able to see the edge of Puerto Rico. Sometimes when relatives called me during the winter and asked what we were doing, I would say, "Lexi and I are hanging out at the beach. It's so nice out here!"

Figure 3: My Community Pool

Figure 4: My Community Gazebo

Chapter Two

Preparing for Irma

When Hurricane Irma was forecast, I was a little in denial. Some natives of the US Virgin Islands told me that a hurricane lands there every three years on average. The Atlantic Hurricane Season begins on June 1st and ends November 30th. During 2016, the number of hurricanes and tropical storms had stirred up in the Atlantic Ocean exceeded its historical average rate. However, they ended up going in different directions from the US Virgin Islands. We experienced some heavy rain instead. I counted those missed hurricanes, and I thought the likelihood of a hurricane within the few years I planned to be in Saint Thomas was low.

During August 2017, meteorologists issued a warning. The storm was growing, they said, and there was a chance of it becoming a category 5 hurricane, which is the most dangerous level. The wind speed of a category 5 hurricane is at least 157 miles per hour. There is no category higher than that. Then, during the last week of August, it was broadcasted that Irma was coming to the US Virgin Islands and that it might hit us directly. Residents started boarding up their homes and closing their hurricane shutters—window shutters specifically meant to protect the glass during hurricanes. My daughter and I lived in a beautiful studio on the first floor, and we cleared our porch and balcony of items so that the hurricane wouldn't pick up the objects and damage our apartment with them.

I felt sort of lost on the topic of hurricanes. My employer distributed literature about safety precautions for hurricanes and I could recall a few things I knew about preparing for tornadoes back in Alabama. Whenever hurricanes made landfalls, the worst parts of those storms usually went around the cities where I lived. I wanted to get a perspective from someone who experienced hurricanes. I walked outside and stood on my porch to get some fresh air and think. When I did, I saw the maintenance worker. So, I asked the maintenance worker what he usually did for hurricanes.

The maintenance worker in my neighborhood made a few suggestions. He recommended that I get a portable stove and some gas canisters and prepare like I was going on a camping trip. So in addition to stocking up on flashlight batteries and canned goods, I went and bought a portable stove. Since there was a high chance that certain restaurants and other merchants would not be in business after the hurricane, I came up with a few more ideas. One idea was stocking up on food from McDonalds. I bought about five orders of pancake-and-sausage breakfasts and froze them. Another idea was buying wireless gadgets. I bought some wireless chargers from AT&T and made sure they were fully charged. I listened closely to the radio for daily weather updates and checked my cell phone regularly.

I asked my landlord whether it would be safe to stay in the apartment. During a hurricane, it is recommended that people stay in concrete buildings instead of wood ones, and my place was made of wood. He answered that the apartments had held up very well during Hurricane Hugo, which was a category 4, but that it was hard to say because it depended on whether the hurricane hit us directly. I became worried. If I decided to leave my apartment, I definitely would not go into a community shelter, especially not after what I had heard about the experience of some of the females survivors of Hurricane Katrina in Louisiana. I had watched a documentary about victims who were sharing their experiences during Hurricane Katrina. One of the women stated that there were many sexual assaults even inside the shelter in broad daylight. I felt I'd rather die than live with that emotional scar.

I talked to family and friends, and they said that it would be better to be safe than sorry. I called around and asked coworkers and the police department for options in case our apartment was ruined during the storm, but I still had no intention of going into a shelter. No one had much information. They all said that shelters would become available as needed and announcements would be made. I thought, "How smart and proactive is that?" I understood that some buildings could be destroyed, but a list should still have been generated so the public would already be aware of the alternatives if those buildings became inhabitable during the storm.

About three days before the storm reached the island, my good friend Steph texted me. She had retired a few months earlier in March, and I thought she had left the island. However, she hadn't, and she offered me and Lexi a place to stay during Irma. She said that she lived in a concrete building about two miles higher up the mountain from me, which was an ideal place for shelter. Oh, it was like music to my ears. Steph said that she had been through various types of storms during her lifetime including blizzards. Although this was going to her first hurricane experience, she felt well prepared for it.

To give a little background about how I knew that I was in danger and should accept Steph's offer, I would like to share something before I go into the next part of the story. I was fortunate to have a godmother as I was growing up. My late godmother could be described as an elderly, upright, righteous person who reminded me somewhat of a good nun. Regardless of what situation she found herself in, her behavior or demeanor remained unchanged. She was not rich, but the level of faith she demonstrated was parallel to that of Job in the Bible. When I was a young child, I felt like I could talk to her about anything because she corrected me when needed in a way that did not make me feel bad about my mistake.

I used to talk to my godmother about these intense feelings I would get when I felt that something bad was going to happen. I told her that I would eventually leave the scene after getting tired of trying to convince people to believe me. And whenever something bad did happen after I left—such as serious arguments or fighting—I would still feel bad afterward because I had known but couldn't do anything to prevent it from happening. I kept asking her to please explain to me why and what I was experiencing because I did not understand the point of having feelings if I could not change the situation. One day my godmother stopped dodging my question and admitted that she could not relate to what I was saying, but she could give me a hint. I said, "Okay." Grinding her teeth as she talked, she very hesitantly said that what I experienced was similar to something called "premonitions." Many years later, only a year prior to the release of this book, I found out through experienced religious leaders that what I was experiencing was related to the gift of discernment, which is listed in 1 Corinthians 12:10, and I was supposed to allow the Holy Spirit to guide me for my protection (John 16:13).

When the storm was about three days away, I experienced a very strong emotion; I believe it was the Holy Spirit warning me that something terrible was going to happen if I continued to live there. That was all I needed in order to decide whether I should stay or leave my apartment. I got everything packed up for me and Lexi. I put her in the car, grabbed our suitcase of essential tools, ran out of the house, and drove up the hill to meet my friend. As I was leaving, I noticed one of my neighbors looking left, right, and to the sky to figure out why I was running. She could not figure it out. It was beyond her understanding.

Steph kindly welcomed us and had everything planned out well. She had plenty of food and a good variety of it. She had tools and even fun things for Lexi to do. We began closing the hurricane shutters and moving furniture off the balcony because it could be lifted by the strong winds and strike the apartment building. The very heavy items, such as the furniture, were placed into storage by Steph's apartment maintenance worker and other male tenants in the apartment building. The rest of the items were put inside the apartments. We filled the freezer and the portable coolers with a lot of ice to try to preserve drinks and perishable items as much as possible. I went into my room and prayed. I was saying the affirmation of faith and planning to recite Psalm 23 afterward, but near the end of my affirmation of faith, I received an answer from God through one of His messengers saying, "Whoa. Don't worry. It's not your time."

Irma Is Here

On the morning of September 6, 2017—one of my favorite coworker's birthdays—the sky began to darken. It started off as a rainstorm but got worse that afternoon. This was the moment when we had all been preparing for. The governor, Kenneth Mapp, warned the members of the community not to go outside and not to be fooled by sudden quiet moments because the high winds were unpredictable, and the situation could be life threatening. He also informed tourists that this was not the time to go surfing at the beach to take advantage of the waves. He emphasized the level of danger that the weather officials had reported: Irma was a category 5 hurricane.

That afternoon, the weather conditions became severe. I got on Facebook and told my family that Hurricane Irma had landed and that we would lose communication temporarily if the power lines and phone towers get destroyed. The airport had canceled flights due to the approaching hurricane. Of course, my family was very worried, but I was as prepared as I could be.

During the storm, the hardest part for me was keeping Lexi calm. Her behavior was similar to a lot of other toddlers—she had so much energy. I figured it would be difficult to keep her still throughout the hurricane. She was too young to comprehend the level of danger we were in, so she whined a lot about sitting in one place for a long period of time. Steph's apartment building consisted of about six apartments, and all the tenants remained during the storm. One of the neighbors was a nurse. The neighbors were very considerate and checked to see whether everyone had what they needed. At one point Lexi was acting so anxious that I said to myself, "If the nurse comes up here and asks me again whether I need something, I'm going to ask her if she has a straitjacket."

The storm started. Steph and I tried to keep Lexi preoccupied as much as possible with coloring activities, books, and toys. Later that day, Lexi became restless and began to move around way too much, and I had to stop her. She didn't like not being able to run around freely, and she began to be defiant. She whined and screamed when I tried to restrict her movement. Eventually, her behavior actually bothered me more than the storm. I began to use a technique that a pediatric dentist had taught me for a child who does not remain still during toothbrushing. I turned her so she faced away from me and wrapped my legs and arms around her. She continued to cry, but she did not understand the extent of danger we were in, so I did what I had to do.

Steph gave me a choice to stay in the inner hallways or the guest bedroom closet with food, drinks, and sheets. I chose the closet. I grabbed some flashlights, personal items, and a pillow, and I created a cool hangout atmosphere with Lexi in the closet. It worked. She remained calm. The guest bedroom had windows. I already knew that during tornado situations, it is best to remain away from windows because they could break. From what I was told by the natives about the nature of hurricanes, if the hurricane creates an opening, it can act as a vacuum and pull out whatever is in the room or area. Since the guest bedroom had windows, Steph offered me a mattress to be placed against the closet door. I accepted and tested its weight by pushing against it when I opened the door in case we had to get out. Since I still felt light airflow that traveled into the closet from underneath the door, and the mattress was not too heavy, I let it stay.

Within a few hours, water began to enter the closet, so I called Steph to remove the mattress. I could have moved it myself if push came to shove, but I did not want to sleep on a wet mattress if I could avoid it. I wanted to place it back on the box spring, and we did. However, there was about a half inch of water in the apartment. Lexi and I then moved to the hallway area with Steph and set up a chair recliner. She asked me whether I had

Figure 5: My Studio Apartment after Hurricane Irma

tightened the window seals. I told her that I made sure they were very tight. Steph took a closer look at the windows and discovered the problem was the shutters. All the water was coming through the shutters. Steph got sheets and tried to soak up some of the water, and we placed a stack of pillows at the edge of the hallway. The glass French doors located in the living room lost their shutters. On the right side of the hallway was the kitchen, which led to the front entrance door of the apartment. We were located on the second level of a three-floor apartment building.

It seemed like forever and a day, but Lexi eventually calmed down as we relaxed in the chair recliner in the inner hallway of the apartment. Steph had a hand-crank radio and listened to it until the radio station shut down. The local radio host was on the air to give the public a sense of comfort through the upcoming disaster. The host opened the line for questions from the community as mother nature allowed. After a period of time, the power went out, then the internet connection. I used an old-school solar hand-crank radio to listen to the radio station until they stopped broadcasting.

When it got very dark, Steph and I took out our flashlights. There were puzzles and plenty of books to read, but none of that was entertaining enough to keep my mind off what was happening. My cell phone battery was fully charged, along with a backup portable battery I had bought from my cell phone provider's store. The more I sat there, the more nervous I became about whether I would have enough battery charge to make it through the storm, so I turned my phone off from time to time, especially when the signal was lost. The whistling sounds from the high winds would stop, then suddenly come on strong again. After a few hours, we were so tired we went to sleep.

The next morning, the storm was still going. It was scary for me to even leave the hallway to go into the kitchen to get something to eat. If your coach ever had you play a sprinting game where he would hold a timer, then have you sprint to a certain cone or object and sprint back to the starting point, that was what it felt like for me. I would first sit and decide on exactly what I wanted to grab to eat or drink for me or Lexi. Then I would run to get it and sprint back to my shut-in spot in the hallway.

Chapter Four

Results of Irma

After the hurricane hit, Steph explained the reason she walked into the living room and stopped and stared during the storm. She said that she had noticed the window shutter kept banging loudly; she was contemplating walking on the balcony to grab it and throw it over the balcony. She figured because of her weight, she would probably be okay. I said I was glad she didn't because that was very risky. Even though she was heavy, that wind was strong enough to pick her up and throw her over the balcony instead.

One of my siblings said that when they had tried to contact the Red Cross concerning my safety and whereabouts, the Red Cross stated they were not able to reach me to confirm because the roads were impassable, which was true. They also told my sister that since I was a foreigner, I would be hard to trace. There were four people reported dead.

We went outside after the storm had passed. A lot of networks were down so we were not able to use our cell phones. For some reason, one of Steph's neighbors, the nurse, was able to send texts via her mobile phone provider—one that was not commonly used on the island. She offered everyone in the apartment building the opportunity to contact someone to let them know that we were safe. I texted one of my sisters, and she passed on the message to the rest of the family, mostly via Facebook. Of course, they were relieved.

Prior to the storm, Steph told me that her landlord said that residents had first choice for vehicle parking spaces. Since I was a visitor, I had to move my car to an area of the apartment building's parking space that was more open and exposed. Thus, I was nervous as I walked to the parking lot to see the condition of my car after the storm. As I walked around it, I noticed minor scratches on the paint, which was trivial.

Then, I saw a loose wire from a nearby power line lying on the hood. One of my neighbors moved the loose wire with his bare hand—which was highly not recommended—off the hood of my car. I looked at his wife and told her I appreciated the thoughtfulness, but that it wasn't a good idea. I remembered that wood is a good nonconductive material. Using a stick to move the possibly live wire would have been safer for both of us.

Steph said she wanted to show me something. She said it was good that I had not parked near the vehicles that were located in the reserved tenant area. Then, she pointed to the cars that were in the reserved area. Most of those cars were damaged, with dents and broken glass. Yet, my car along with other tenants' vehicles that were parked next to mine in the exposed area were not damaged.

I was expecting to see dents, or my car even being flipped over. Some of the homeowners who were fortunate to have car garages reported that their garages collapsed on top of their vehicles. I thanked God my car was still in good cosmetic and mechanical condition. I had filled the gas tank prior to the storm, so later I was able to drive anywhere I needed to go on the island. After I drove my car around a few miles, the excess water came out of the lines, and it operated more smoothly. Although power lines and trees had fallen across the road, some people navigated their vehicles around the obstacles, took pictures of the island, and made videos with their cell phones. However, the road and its surrounding view did not look the same. Sometimes I ordered pizza by use of landmarks and distance given to the food deliver. I was thinking until the island restored, it would be confusing for someone who depended on landmarks and trees instead of street signs to get from one place to another. The road view was so unrecognizable, a driver would probably second-guess their route. The commercial airport in Saint Thomas was severely damaged. No commercial airplanes could fly in or out. The port for the sea planes was also broken.

I drove down the street to see my apartment. It was not in a fortunate position. My apartment had very heavy sliding wood doors that covered the front and side of the apartment. Both doors had come off, and the furniture inside was shifted due to the wind. It was scary to think what that would have been like if we had stayed in our apartment. I had been told an upstairs apartment was a better option than a downstairs apartment in these types of conditions. However, the upstairs apartment was in even worse condition than mine. Glass was everywhere. I was afraid and tried to call my neighbor. I received no answer. I found his girlfriend's mobile number stored in my phone from the time we had to purchase water for our cistern when it ran out of water. She said they were stateside when the hurricane struck, and he was okay. I sent her pictures of their apartment and told her to tell him that his Jeep was in good condition. She asked for pictures of his vehicle, and I forwarded them to her as well.

As people evacuated the island, Steph researched, applied, and networked to get her cruise line ticket. One day, she walked into the apartment upset. She said her plans of leaving the island had been delayed. Steph explained that although she had a boarding pass, the staff denied her the opportunity to travel because they doubted whether her health condition was stable enough for her to withstand the trip. Steph mentioned that she had doubts that the cruise ship was fully booked as announced because she saw at least two empty seats before she was turned away.

Chapter Five

Tropical Storm José

During the time Hurricane Irma was leaving, another hurricane was traveling within the Atlantic Ocean: category 4 José. By the time it reached the US Virgin Islands, the winds had diminished, and it made landfall as a tropical storm.

The only advantage the people in Steph's apartment building saw to Tropical Storm José was that it replenished the water that was lost in the swimming pool from Hurricane Irma picking it up. The tenants took water jugs and other containers down to the pool and filled them with rainwater from the pool. I helped people carry water to their own and Steph's apartments. We used the jug water then for manually flushing the toilets since we had no electricity or running water. For personal hygiene, Lexi and I both used baby wipes. Until my bottled water supply ran out, I used it sparingly for drinking, brushing teeth, and washing hands when necessary.

Figure 6: Steph and Lexi

After the end of José, I noticed something about Lexi really amazed me—her level of adaptability or resilience. She used to watch TV every day and played with electronic gadgets and teleconferenced her dad prior to the storms. I thought that she would not do well with an overnight manual lifestyle change. This was one time I was glad that I was wrong. Steph read books to her. Steph told me that she noticed one book that she loved because Lexi wanted her to read it to her repeatedly. I picked it up and read it to Lexi regularly from that point. We also played games with her. Steph poured a lot of building blocks and colorful toys in the middle of the living room floor, and it became like a playland to Lexi. I thought Lexi would request and cry over not seeing cartoons, but she did not. I remember how much I liked balloons when I was a child, and I told Steph. Steph said she had a few balloons too. As Steph began to blow up the balloons, Lexi became very focused on them. Some of them popped, and Lexi could barely wait until Steph was finished blowing up the next balloon. Lexi smiled and bounced the balloons in the air around the apartment because I told her not to let it hit the floor or it might pop.

Lexi got bored sometimes, but it happened no more than another kid who got bored from playing with one video game and wanted another one. Steph said she had another idea. When Steph pulled out a bubble solution and blew bubbles, Lexi yelled, "Bubble party!" And there was vibrant Lexi, screaming in her iconic voice with excitement as she chased the bubbles. I cracked the French door to get more wind inside for the bubbles. Sometimes, the wind was a little strong, so I had to gauge the crack from time to time. When the weather returned to its normal condition, she and I blew bubbles over the balcony and watched them float away. My thoughts were that Lexi did not miss the technology-related activities as much because she preferred in-person interaction. She valued my undivided attention.

Chapter Six

Aftermath of Irma

Public officials set a curfew for safety reasons. During the day, the city workers were supposed to work on the roads early in the morning until around nine or ten o'clock. Then the rest of the citizens could get on the roads to go and get supplies from the store or free services, such as from military personnel. Suppliers would run out, and unfortunately, residents would have to return the next day and stand in the hot sun in long lines. Suppliers included business owners as well as military personnel. Some of the people waiting had other family members to feed. In addition to rations, there were care packages provided by a senior citizen organization, but there was a lot of traffic in the relatively short window of time given by local authorities to get the supplies you needed.

Sometimes I drove around to find a strong telecommunication signal. Then, I sent messages or made phone calls. One place was not always a reliable location. Prior to the storm, I had taken the proper precautions and filled up my car with gas. However, when the gas tank got low, it was hectic trying to get a refill. Cars and people were lined up in the direct sunlight for about an hour, and then gas needed to be carried from the pump by hand. It was hard for people who were alone. Yet, I was with my three-year-old running errands in the hot weather, which made it an even more stressful task.

The residents were informed that the community would have conferences by radio, and it was very important that we tune in at a scheduled time of day to get important updates. As mentioned before, Steph had a solar hand-crank radio. I would place it on the balcony in the sunlight sometimes. It was operated by manually winding it up, and then you could listen to what was on the radio. Other than that, I would go out into the parking lot and turn on the car radio to listen to the local radio station for updates on rations, public announcements, and the scheduled press conferences.

Some businesses raised the prices of commodities such as water and ice. Oh my God, ice was very hard to find! Due to my educational background in business, I understood the concept of supply and demand. However, the problem I had was when local business owners raised the price of supplies to more than double the original prices after a catastrophic event, which was illegal. During the radio conference, Governor Mapp addressed this problem and told the business owners to stop price gouging. He urged the community that if we experienced any more price gouging to please report those activities to authorities.

Governor Mapp said that he had the honor to speak with President Donald Trump. President Trump sent a message specifically to the US Virgin Islands saying that he loved the people of the US Virgin Islands, and he planned to visit soon to assess the damage from the storm. President Trump sent officers from the New York City Police Department (NYPD) as volunteers to assist the community and was going to send the United States Marines as well, for some reason. I asked myself, "Huh? The marines? Why?" If the United States Marines assisted the community, I never noticed, but I did see members of the United States National Guard.

Figure 7: Airport in Saint Thomas

Figure 8: Cruise line ships

The picture in Figure 8 was taken about a year prior to Hurricane Irma. This is an example of the cruise line ship that I saw people boarding in the aftermath of Hurricane Irma. Numerous people were getting off the island as quickly as they could. In an effort to assist evacuees, there were cruise line companies that offered one-way cruises to Florida for free. The rumor was that people were having a good time on the ships, eating a lot of food and drinking complimentary alcohol, all at the expense of the cruise lines.

I considered boarding one of the cruise ships for Florida, but then I heard someone talking on the radio about the cruise offer, and he warned customers to be aware that the bunks would be shared by any random person. With a three-year-old, I felt uneasy about this arrangement for three reasons. First, Lexi was very friendly and would run away from me every chance she could. Second, I was a single mom in a part of the world that was away from all relatives and friends I knew and trusted. Third,

I wanted to minimize the risk of me or my child becoming a victim of abuse by a stranger, as some women had reported after Hurricane Katrina. Therefore, I figured the arrangement would not be suitable for me and my child, and I decided to wait for the airport to be repaired to leave the island via airplane.

Well, God wanted to show me something else. So I could not leave. Instead of the airplane, Maria arrived first.

Chapter Seven

Preparing for Maria

Even though I remembered what one of my sisters said had happened when she contacted the Red Cross to find me, I went to Red Cross. They were set up outside in the plaza. I introduced myself and presented my identification. I asked them whether they could update my records because they stated that I was a foreigner. I told the worker that I was not a foreigner because I was a US citizen, and the US Virgin Islands were part of US territory. Yet the Red Cross representative repeated that I was a foreigner, so she could not help me.

Then I told her I had not come to argue with her; I had come to introduce myself and try to update their system for the purpose of tracking, because I was not leaving with the tourists. I said I had decided to stay on the island and prepare for the next hurricane. She sat very still, and her eyes widened. I left. I told one of my coworkers that the Red Cross volunteer had said she could not help me and that she gave me an odd look when I mentioned Hurricane Maria. I said she looked at me as though she did not know about Hurricane Maria heading this way. My coworker said she probably didn't.

The next time I saw some of the Red Cross volunteers, they were standing outside. They barely let me get two sentences out before saying they could not help me. I didn't know why and did not even try to take the time to analyze the reason the Red Cross volunteers reacted that way toward me. I was persistent and told them I just wanted to ask them one question. It immediately became noisy outside, so I asked the volunteers individually whether they knew about Hurricane Maria. They all answered no.

Then one of the volunteers stepped forward and said they could not help me with the plane situation but would like to offer me an opportunity to leave with them on the ferry. They pointed to Crown Bay Marina. I knew that dock location was not used by commercial cruise ships. Only ferries, boats, and yachts used that port. Then, they said it was very important that I was in place at a certain time because the offer was on a first-come, first-served basis. I told them I would think about it. When it was close to the scheduled departure time, I contacted them via phone to thank them for the offer and informed them that I had decided to stay. They asked why. I told them I would rather wait for the airplane and did not want to carry my daughter out in the middle of all that chaos. They said, "Okay. It's your decision, and we have to respect that." I felt like I had made the right decision, though.

"At least we have been through this before," I thought.

Steph decided to take a ship from the Majesty of the Seas cruise line to get off the island and was successful. Her apartment was paid up for about one to two months, so she offered that we could stay there until the lease ended, or I could take up the lease. Her landlord said she would be okay with that arrangement. I accepted Steph's offer to stay in her apartment only until the end of her lease.

Even during times of obvious hardship on the island, tenants were harassed. There were people complaining about their landlords threatening to evict them if they did not pay their rent—even though their places were uninhabitable. A person who was knowledgeable about real estate law broadcasted on the radio that the reports they had received regarding landlords were illegal. The radio guest speaker said that a landlord could not evict their tenant during a natural disaster and urged victims to report their landlord if they continued to be threatened to be evicted for non-payment of the rent.

As I was in a conversation with a landlord, he mentioned his point of view of the situation of rent. The landlord claimed that his merchants and bank lenders had not been as lenient as he expected they would be. The landlord's wife assisted him with the operation of the apartment building. She was also standing there during the conversation, and she concurred. Although the merchant and bank lender were aware of the natural disaster, they did not allow a reasonable period of time to recover. Instead, they resumed billing and requested payments from the landlord for the apartment building, and they did not know what to do.

An odd thing happened as I was praying for protection against the next storm—Hurricane Maria. As I began to pray, I felt like something bad was going to happen in Puerto Rico. I was so sad, and I began crying. I did not understand the feeling because I was also getting ready to be hit by the same storm. I posted on Facebook that I had a bad feeling about Puerto Rico.

Even though Steph was gone, I felt I had learned what I needed to know. I knew the drill. Just as I had prepared for Hurricane Irma, I made sure that everything on the balcony and porch was moved to an indoor location. I used extra towels and sheets as lining for the windows and doors. For Lexi's safety, I placed a group of pillows as if they were a stack of sandbags to help Lexi know when she could not walk any farther.

Chapter Eight

Maria Is Here

I began to hear a whistling sound from the wind. It got stronger, and I became nervous. My daughter and I sheltered in place again as we had before. I got on Facebook and told my family and friends that Maria was now on the way. One of my cousins posted, "He did it before. He will do it again." His reminder helped increase my level of faith.

I had experience from the first hurricane, so that also helped me not feel like a newbie. As far as natural disasters go, I had previously only prepared for tornadoes back in Alabama, and they had usually passed by our city. When a hurricane came, usually Florida took the big hit, and Alabama would only get heavy rain or a relatively small number of fallen trees or powerlines down on the back end.

Steph, on the other hand, had experience with a variety of storms during her lifetime, so she was like a Girl Scout troop leader to me, showing me the ropes on how to deal with nature with very few resources. And she had done a good job of teaching me; I felt more equipped with the survival skills that she had showed me.

I also felt safer, of course, with confirmation from Jesus that I would live. Yet, I was physically and mentally exhausted from the preparations for Hurricane Maria, so I held my hands up and said, "Jesus, take the wheel." I went to sleep on a reclining chair with Lexi close by. I slept through most of the storm. Lexi became a bit restless, so I tried to keep her distracted with activities like coloring as I did before when Irma came.

I knew when the storm was right around Steph's apartment building because I would feel its energy. Suddenly, a very loud annoying sound went into my ears. It sounded the way the TVs did during 1980s when no more programs were available and vertical multistripes came on the TV screen. My ears became so clogged. I could not hear anything out of my right ear; I could hear partially out of my left ear. I wondered if I was going to go partially deaf. It weakened me. I became so unbalanced I grabbed the chair to keep from falling on the floor, because a collapse on the concrete floor would not have been good. I covered Lexi's ears just in case she felt the same sensation from the hurricane. Then I stuffed her ears with pieces of tissue. and she fell asleep. Many years ago, I was taught on my first plane ride to London that I could chew gum or stuff my ears with ear plugs when they feel abnormal. I had neither of those items. Instead, I moved my jaws in a motion as if I had chewing gum, and I covered my ears. That helped.

I began praying. Then I remember what God told me. I believed it the first time, but my faith increased during Maria, and I believed what he said to me more than ever. I began to regain strength; then, the storm began to rage. I stood up and my feet were wet. I felt the breeze from all the cracks in the doors and windows coming down the hall toward me. The inside and outside doors were shaking very fast. Still, I lifted I hands up to the heavens. Remembering when Jesus was with his disciplines in Matthew 8:23–27, I acknowledged the power of the Lord over the storm. Then I began to sing the lyrics from "Through the Storm" by Yolanda Adams. It made me feel so much better. I grabbed some linen to help soak up the water, then I relaxed and fell back to sleep. The storm lasted about one day.

Chapter Nine

Results of Maria

The US Virgin Islands took a big hit from category 5 Hurricane Maria. This second hit was within two weeks of Irma. People in the community said that we had taken two hits and that we would not be able to survive another one. However, Governor Mapp kept a positive attitude and reassured the public that the US Virgin Islands would heal, would rebuild, and that after reconstruction the islands' structures would be in even better condition than before the hurricanes.

People within the Saint Thomas community suggested that the wires be buried in the ground to prevent electrical and telecommunication damages in the future. No promises were made in an attempt to make that happen. The storm was strong enough to set the island back further and delay my plans to leave the island.

The progress in airport repairs that had been made after Irma was ruined by Maria. The roof of the airport was damaged, so there were leaks, and the machines inside the airport were also damaged. As a result, I was not able to leave the island, and my level of frustration and disappointment increased. Puerto Rico was also hit hard by Maria at a category 4. It was all over the news. Many places were flooded. There was no electricity on the whole island except for the few fortunate residents who had generators. People there were devastated.

Prior to the storms, there had been talk about Puerto Rico becoming the fifty-first state instead of being a US territory. Those thoughts and proposals faded after Maria. There had already been hesitancy about the state proposal due to the level of debt that was owed by Puerto Rico. If that were true, then I guessed the storm, on top of that matter, caused them to be viewed as even more of a liability.

Chapter Ten

Aftermath of Maria

The effects of Maria were quite interesting. Imagine you have money, but you can't spend it. When many places of businesses were severely damaged, people's jobs were destroyed, or they were laid off until further notice. Yet, they did not have the advantage of insurance to allow them to get paid after the catastrophic event. Because I was a salaried employee, I was one of the few fortunate ones to still be electronically compensated during closed times. But for a period of time, there was little or no electricity or telecommunication. Therefore, banking was a problem. The situation sort of reminded me of what actors from the classic show *Gilligan's Island* experienced. I had money in the bank, but could not spend it!

When there was bank access, there were long lines at the ATM outside the bank. People had to get there quickly because it would run out of bills. The merchants' cash registers were down, so cash was all the business owners could accept. At one of the banks, there were guards posted for security at the ATMs with what appeared to be machine guns.

Out of all the houses and apartments buildings within my gated community, my apartment building was the one that got damaged the most. Federal Emergency Management Agency (FEMA) came out to my property to view and evaluate the damages. My daughter was with me at that point; she could not remain still and wanted to walk around, and she would cry if I let her sit in the car while the FEMA representative and I did a walk-through. She said to the FEMA representative, "Wow, somebody needs to clean up!"

When I saw Lexi begin to get comfortable skipping around, I told her to stop and that she could not even walk fast because there were no doctors on the island. (There were people who said the doctors left the island on planes, private or not.) Besides that, the appointment with the FEMA representative went smoothly.

Prior to the FEMA inspection, some neighbors had bragged about the insurance they had and how they were okay. After the evaluation, some of my neighbors looted my apartment. Ironically, the neighbor who was bragging during the day about how he was okay because of his home insurance and FEMA assistance was the main one the maintenance worker caught looting. The looters told him that the homeowner's association assistant president had told them that they could. The maintenance man and I went to his apartment and confronted him over it and filed a police report against him. After about a week, the maintenance worker called me and told me that he wanted to show me something. I went and saw that the looters had returned my items.

Due to the lack of electricity, most chores needed to be done by hand, including washing clothes. When Lexi noticed her clothes hung out to dry around our property, she rushed to pick them up. I worked hard to keep Lexi occupied and having fun so that I would not have to look at her sad facial expression. She did not say a word, but I heard her when she made a subtle sound of disappointment. She did not know how to express some of thoughts in words, so I read her nonverbal cues.

Figure 9: Lexi during laundry time

There were some serious concerns raised about the location of the local correctional facility and the public's safety against the prisoners. Thus, the inmates ended up getting relocated. The NYPD reported to the US Virgin Islands. They assisted with maintaining order. If they served on Saint Thomas, I did not see them. I heard that the local police officers along with the governor did some things that were not ethical, such as favoritism, but I won't get into that. It was addressed by a judge, and Governor Mapp offered a public apology to the community for those acts. There was a reasonable amount of reporting or news coverage after Irma, but the national news coverage significantly decreased for the US Virgin

Islands during after Maria occurred. Many residents within the USVI were feeling emotions of abandonment because their community was not covered on the nationwide news. Although they expressed those concerns, there were reporters at a press conference who alleged they could not cover the US Virgin Islands because they were hindered by the authorities despite having a pass. I was not sure whether the reporters were referring to the local law enforcement, NYPD, or the Department of Defense. But Governor Mapp stated he had no knowledge of the reporters' restrictions. He offered an apology to the reporters and made it clear to the involved authorities that access should have been granted if they had a pass. After that point, the press had the access they needed to report on the status of the communities of the US Virgin Islands.

Besides that, I was so impressed with the contribution of the US Army National Guard and Army Corps of Engineers. I saw them work hard, and I was very proud of how they served the community. There was a list of residents who had roof damage. The National Guard seemed more approachable in problem-solving issues with the residents. If someone complained that their roof was not repaired even though they had signed up much earlier than others, the National Guard took the time to talk with them and explained that requests were granted based on priority. For example, if the percentage of roof damage of a neighbor's home was higher than the home of the complaining resident, the National Guard would place a tarp on the home with the most critical damage first.

Speaking of repairs, the community was warned by authorities of possible scams and people taking advantage of vulnerable homeowners in need of repairs and even claiming they were FEMA representatives, so we needed to be wary of those types of transactions. Besides repairing roofing, the National Guard issued food rations (MRE) and other essential supplies until the supplies ran out for the day.

As I was doing transactions with some business owners, they counterargued that they were not the bad guys and were helping the community by operating during curfew hours because the time restrictions were too strict. I would like to note here that during the early stages of the COVID-19 pandemic, elderly people were at a disadvantage, and business owners designated times for the elderly to shop for supplies for that reason. I thought that was very considerate, and I really wished during the aftermath of the hurricanes that I was given the same consideration as a mom with a toddler. I felt vulnerable walking around with Lexi, and it was so hot sometimes that I carried an umbrella in Lexi's diaper bag. When were stuck in long lines, standing outside in direct sunlight, I pulled out the umbrella and a bottle of water out of Lexi's diaper bag that was sitting in the cooler overnight. We drank some of the water and I poured some of it in my hand, then sprinkled it on us.

I am not advocating breaking the law. I'm just saying that some residents violated curfew to buy items from business owners in order to avoid congestion from the crowds and to avoid standing in very hot weather for long periods of time. Since the residents would not stop participating in buying items, Governor Mapp then threatened to issue citations and monetary fines to those businesses that were selling items past curfew. If the violations continued, he warned that it could result in loss of business. Another reason people violated curfew was because they wanted to help clean up the community. Yet the power lines were live, so authorities saw the resident volunteers' gestures as more of a risk and continued to urge them to stay inside until the maintenance crews finished working and the curfew was lifted.

Figure 10: Airport in Saint Thomas

Chapter Eleven

Going Home

When I went to the airport, it did not go smoothly. When I arrived, the Transportation Security Administration (TSA) Representative said the emergency flights were only available for evacuees with serious medical conditions at that time. I was diagnosed with one of the medical conditions on their printed list. Then I said I had a minor child with me, we lost our home, and I would like to travel back to my hometown. The TSA Rep did not seem sympathetic at all. She told me that I needed medical proof. I left to get medical documentation and returned to the airport. Then the TSA Rep told me that now I had to show proof that I was stable enough to board the plane and that I need to show medications. I told her that I was out of medication and from what I had heard, there were no doctors available on the island. She said she could not allow me on the plane then and that I could possibly speak with a pharmacist for a refill. The problem was that my prescription had recently expired.

I went back to my health care provider and told them what the airport representative said. My health care provider told me that since my prescription had expired, I would need another evaluation before another prescription could be issued. I asked when a doctor would be available. They said no doctors were there, and it would be about two weeks before they could see me. After I explained my living situation, they gave me a medical note to take to a pharmacist and said it would be up to the pharmacist to honor it.

I left and went to the pharmacist. The line was so long that people were outside the drug store. It was a pharmacy, so I did expect to wait awhile anyway. I knew that a one-hour wait, though, was hard on Lexi. I usually made sure that she was dry and fed and that I had at least one snack and drink on hand before trying to conduct business along with her. After I had stood in line for an hour, the pharmacist looked at my medical history and told me he would grant me one extension of a thirty-day supply for the flight, and my doctor would have to take it from there. I was grateful and said that was fair enough, and I headed back to the airport in my hot car.

The errands I had experienced reminded me of what Steph told me when she was initially rejected by the cruise line due to instability of her health condition when she first arrived with a boarding pass. When I arrived back at the airport, I was hot and sweating. I had a feeling that things were still not going to go well once I got inside the airport. The thought that I became homeless with a minor child with me did not make a difference to them made me angry. As we walked in the door registration window, everyone in the lobby became quiet. When people who were standing in line looked at me, they voluntarily stepped out of line. I presented my photo ID again with medical proof and medication to the TSA Rep. The representative stepped back and said she didn't need to see the medication bottle. She said I could sign the waiting list, but they must evaluate the case and if they make a favorable decision, they will call me when a flight becomes available.

Then I said to the TSA Rep, "Can I speak to your supervisor?" Then both of them stood there behind the window. I stated the situation to her supervisor and questioned the policies. Her supervisor's responses seemed unreasonable. Then I spoke candidly. I said, "You all are hassling me."

They responded, "No, it is how the process works."

I said, "I've been patient as long as I know how to be, but you all are hassling me. I'm not a tourist. I showed you my local driver license. I am a resident here." Then I pulled out my Social Security Administration badge and said, "I served *your* community, and this is how you repay me along with my child? If I *am* unstable, it is due to the severe weather, the living conditions, and your unreasonable rules and policies."

One of the customers who stepped out of line was an elderly man, and he was standing behind me and said with subtlety, "You all need to help her." Then the TSA representative said they had to verify the information and would give me a call.

I said, "Y'all need to think about the way you all treat people. If you don't, when people finally get off this island, they will think twice before coming this way again. And how would your revenue begin to look then? Not good."

During the heated conversation between me and the TSA staff member, military personnel stepped forward in my direction. By the time I turned around to leave, they stepped back in front of the door. Then I said to them, "I hope you all took good mental notes of this. Do you all think this is right?" I continued, "I served this country too." Then the military personnel began to take steps backward. I told them, "My name is Senedtra Cowan, and I am a US Army veteran." I presented my ID cards. They looked at them, handed them back to me, and stepped aside as Lexi and I walked out of the airport. Then I said to myself, "I did my part. I am going have to put this in the Lord's hands."

We missed some flight opportunities due to word-of-mouth communication given about flight availability. By the time the flight announcements were broadcast, they would say the seats were already taken. Steph's apartment building was located near the airport, so I was able to see every plane leave and would wonder how we had missed the communication.

Finally, one day when I called, I insisted on a date and time being given to me.

The airplane that we finally took home was not through the airline that I had planned, but I made sure that we got on it. My neighbors drove us to the airport. The airline was JetBlue. Members of the community who were high-enough priority were offered a complimentary flight from Saint Thomas to Florida due to the state of emergency.

When my daughter and I finally boarded the plane, I began to feel a good sense of relief. I took note of something else. Just as Steph had told me that she had seen extra seats on the cruise ship before being turned away, I also noticed a number of empty seats in different areas while we were traveling on the airplane. I counted about six empty seats.

As I exited the plane, the flight attendant and co-captain were politely standing at the exit. I turned to the co-captain and said, "Oh, thank you for saving us off of Gilligan's Island!"

He laughed and humbly said, "I'm just a man."

From Florida, I called Delta Airlines and requested they change my departure airport from Saint Thomas to Fort Lauderdale because I had taken an emergency flight out. From Florida, Lexi and I flew with Delta Airlines back to Alabama.

Chapter Twelve

Home at Last

While we were in Saint Thomas, a coworker from one of my agency's branches in Florida told my manager that he had heard about the storms. He lived in Florida, but he was originally from Saint Thomas and felt very empathetic and wanted to help someone in need. My branch manager told the employee that Lexi and I could use some help. I answered the phone and told the coworker the size of clothes Lexi wore and the type of toys she liked. So that employee, along with all his coworkers, decided to put together a gift basket. He said he would send it when I reached my destination.

After we arrived in Alabama, the employee from the Florida office called and told me that we would receive a card, gift card, and a box of clothes for my daughter from their staff. When it arrived, watching Lexi open the boxes felt like Christmas. Her face was so lit up. We had arrived in Alabama with only one suitcase and a handbag, so it was amazing that she was sent a full wardrobe of new clothes and I was given a small gift card to help with other essentials.

Figure 11: Lexi and her donated gifts from coworkers in the Florida office

Shortly after that, managers from one of the offices in Puerto Rico got in contact with me to make sure that we were safe during our travels, settled in at home, and situated at a new job location.

As for my car, I did not want to leave it in Saint Thomas. So I had it shipped back to the United States mainland. It arrived about a month after I did. I don't mean to sound materialistic, but I thought of the car as a blessing because it had been shipped to Saint Thomas, survived two major hurricanes without damage, and was shipped back to Alabama

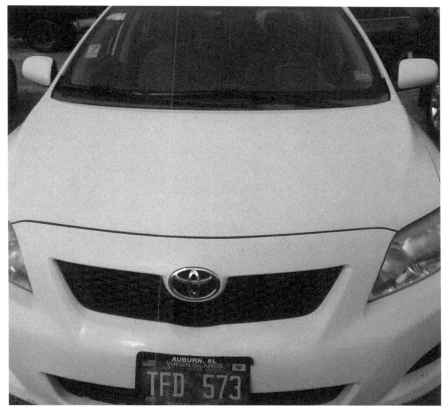

Figure 12: My car at the Bureau of Customs and Border Protection

in good condition. Although it is not a yellow-and-black Camaro, it's *my* "Bumblebee" (like from the Transformers movie franchise). It's a Toyota Corolla.

I remember when I first bought the car. I was still married at the time. The car dealership phoned me, but I missed the call. I was so nervous thinking they were going to make me return the car due to something adverse they had found on my credit. My husband at that time prayed with me about it. When he opened his eyes and looked at me, he said confidently, "The car is yours. They can't take it back."

I kept saying, "Are you sure? Are you sure?" Nothing about his confirmation was shaky. He repeatedly said yes. Wow, the amount of relief that came over me! It may not seem so important to readers who have never lived in poverty, but it was a big deal to me, as I did not have public transportation and was living from paycheck to paycheck.

When I called back, the representative only wanted me to sign some more paperwork. I still have that car about ten years later, and it still runs well. Thus, my car was not just a car to me. It was a blessing from God. I did not want to take it for granted. It was a reminder that the Lord brought me from a mighty long way.

When my car was delivered, the vehicle transporter smiled and unloaded my Toyota with a pleasant manner. I signed for the car, and as I walked away, he stopped me and said, "I need to talk to you. I normally don't do this."

I stopped and listened.

He asked, "Are you a veteran?"

I said, "Yes."

He asked which branch, and I said army. He said, "Me too." Then we had a discussion, and I told him something that had frustrated and puzzled me every time I thought about it for the last 15 years. He told me what I needed to do and insisted that I try; then he left. One day, I did what he suggested, and that information led to the other part of my breakthrough, and I was very happy God had placed him in my path. Sorry, I decided to keep the details of that breakthrough to myself at this time.

Closing Remarks

Lexi has not recalled the events the way I see them because of her lack of maturity at the time. Most of her memories of the island are filled with good times; if she had a chance, she would want to live there again. Given the types of meaningful friendships I made while living on the island, we would like to visit one day. The overall experience has made me see the basic things in life that we often take for granted, such as lights, telecommunication, washing machines, and more.

Some businesses and government agencies may feel as if my account is a source of revenge or expression of resentment. No, I forgave you. I do hope, however, that I have shared something that might inspire ideas that could be used within an area that needs serious improvement.

This book is also a testimony to those who have suffered so much. I hope this book will enlighten and encourage other victims to keep on keeping on. After my period of turmoil, the Lord gave me more than *double* for my *trouble*.

Acknowledgments

People talk about how the Lord has taken care of them through their spiritual storms. I would like to thank God for delivering me through my spiritual storms and sparing me—not once, but twice—through the storms of Hurricane Irma and Hurricane Maria.

Next, I thank those who took the time to pray for us and those who encouraged me to write this book. I also would like to thank my friend Steph and others, including my coworkers, who allowed the Lord to use them in lending a helping hand before, during, and after the storms.

I also would like to acknowledge my English 101 professor from Alabama A&M University, who told me as I was turning in an essay how impressed she was and that I had serious potential to become a writer. Although it was a brief moment in the late nineties, I felt it and carried those sincere words of acknowledgement and encouragement with me.

Figure 13: Palm trees at the beach in Saint Thomas

Lightning Source UK Ltd.
Milton Keynes UK
UKHW051448120223
416624UK00009B/26